Deep Learning for Beginners

A comprehensive introduction of deep learning fundamentals for beginners to understanding frameworks, neural networks, large datasets, and creative applications with ease

Steven Cooper

DATA SCIENCE

ii

creating a secondary or tertiary copy of the work or a recorded copy and is only allowed with express written consent from the Publisher. All additional right reserved.

The information in the following pages is broadly considered to be a truthful and accurate account of facts, and as such, any inattention, use or misuse of the information in question by the reader will render any resulting actions solely under their purview. There are no scenarios in which the publisher or the original author of this work can be in any fashion deemed liable for any hardship or damages that may befall them after undertaking information described herein.

Additionally, the information in the following pages is intended only for informational purposes and should thus be thought of as universal. As befitting its nature, it is presented without assurance regarding its prolonged validity or interim quality. Trademarks that are mentioned are done without written consent and can in no way be considered an endorsement from the trademark holder.

Table of Contents

Preface

The main purpose of this book is to provide the reader with the most elementary knowledge of deep learning fundamentals so that they can understand what these are all about.

Book Objectives

This book will help you:

- Know more about the fundamental principles of deep learning and what different frameworks, networks, and applications exist.

- Have an elementary grasp of deep learning concepts and tools that will make this work easier to do.

- Have achieved a technical background in deep learning and appreciate its power.

x

Target Users

The book is designed for a variety of target audiences. The most suitable users would include:

- Newbies in computer science techniques and deep learning

- Professionals in deep learning and social sciences

- Professors, lecturers or tutors who are looking to find better ways to explain the content to their students in the simplest and easiest way

- Students and academicians, especially those focusing on deep learning and software development

Is this book for me?

This book is for those who are interested in deep learning. There are a lot of skills that a data scientist needs, such as coding, intellectual mindset, eagerness to make new discoveries, and much more.

It's important that you are interested in this because you are obsessed with this kind of work. Little programming experience is required. If you already wrote a few lines of code and recognize basic programming statements, then this book is for you.

Introduction

Deep learning refers to learning approaches that attempt modeling of data with complex forms, combining different non-linear types of transformations. The fundamental building blocks of deep learning are neural networks, which are placed in combination, in order to form deep neural networks. These methods have allowed for significant advancement within the fields of image and sound processing, in technologies such as language processing and facial recognition, automated language processing, and text classification.

The potential applications for this technology are endless. Conventional machine approaches did not have the capacity to process natural data in its raw form. For a number of years, construction of a pattern or machine learning system needed engineering and expertise of the domain to generate the design of feature extractors, which allowed the raw data, that included pixel values, to transform into a suitable facsimile of feature vectors, where the learning system could identify or organize patterns within the input.

As such, this book will consider the essentials of deep learning for novices in the subject, and tackle fundamental lexicon, such as the difference between machine learning, deep learning, and artificial intelligence. The book will also consider the deep learning frameworks which are preferable and available. As the book delves deeper into the concepts, you will be shown how to build various algorithms, like deep convolutional networks, general adversarial networks, and recurrent neural networks. You will also know how to apply the algorithms for exploring creative applications, such as training devices to recognize objects within an image, and the ways to learn deep learning in general.

Deep learning is making advances in explaining issues which have been risky for the artificial intelligence networks. It is good at working out perplexing structures and so can be connected to several applications in science, business, and government. Notwithstanding making fast work of picture and sound assessment issues, it is also being utilized for investigation of particle accelerator information, anticipating the impacts of transformations in DNA arrangements, and foreseeing the movement of test medicated particles. In that capacity, deep learning has thought of as promising outcomes for various assignments in characteristic dialect, particularly when seen with regards to the characterization of points, replying to inquiries, and dialect interpretation. Deep learning will dependably have significantly more accomplishments sooner rather than later as it needs only a small amount of designing by hand, which implies it will exploit on this steady movement to calculation approaches.

Presently, deep learning is an element of machine learning, and these are both identified with man-made brainpower, but what is the difference between, artificial intelligence, machine learning, and deep learning? Artificial intelligence as a term was initiated by John McCarthy in 1956 and involves machines which are able to perform tasks which would be considered as attributes of human intelligence.

That would include things like recognizing and distinguishing objects and sounds, learning, and understanding language. As such, artificial intelligence has become a part of the thought processing slowly developing in academic research settings since the first researchers came up with the term in the Dartmouth conferences. In the decades since that time, artificial intelligence has been heralded as one of those Holy Grails of science, before it was then thrust into technology's problem sets as the be all and end all of accomplishment. Over the past few years, though, artificial intelligence has had further development, and a lot of this enthusiasm has to do with the availability of GPUs which allow for parallel processing in a faster and cheaper manner. This also has to do with the simultaneous one-two punch of infinite storage, and the data of every stripe, including text, video, and geospatial data.

These modalities can be grouped according to narrow and general artificial intelligence. Narrow AI shows facets of human intelligence and can do this well, but it lacks when it comes to other things. A tool which is great at facial recognition, for example, but cannot do much else, would be such an example. General artificial intelligence, on the other hand, has the attributes of human intelligence, such as the attributes mentioned in recognition, processing, and problem-solving.

Machine learning is apparently a means to an end to achieve artificial intelligence. It is allegedly the ability for a tool to learn, without explicitly being programmed. As such, one can have artificial intelligence in a tool without having to use machine learning, though, this would still need a form of intelligence to build millions of lines of code, complete with decision trees. As opposed to hard-coding, the software routines with instructions in order to accomplish every little task, machine learning is a means of training the algorithm so that it can do things by itself. This conditioning of the algorithm entails feeding large amounts of data to the algorithm and allowing it to readjust itself so that it can improve.

As an example here, machine learning has been utilized to make improvements to computer vision. You assemble several photos and then have people tag them. For instance, people can tag pictures with a pet in them as opposed to those who do not. This algorithm tries to construct a model which would accurately tag a picture that has a pet, or not, as well as a person would. Once the level of accuracy has reached the designated base-lines, then the machine has actually learned what a pet looks like.

Deep learning, as the last lexicon which is appropriate to this context, is a part of the approaches to machine learning. There are also other methodologies such as inductive logic programming, reinforcement learning, as well as decision tree learning. Deep learning was inspired by the structure and function of the brain, such as the interconnection of neurons. Artificial neural networks are some of the algorithms similar to the biological structure of the brain.

Chapter 1:
Defining Lexicon and
Related Concepts

Machine learning, artificial intelligence, and deep learning

"Artificial Intelligence, deep learning, machine learning—whatever you're doing if you don't understand it—learn it. Because otherwise you're going to be a dinosaur within 3 years." - **Mark Cuban**

In the most basic terms, deep learning could be explained as a method of probability prediction. Depending on the size of the dataset, the function will be able to make statements, predictions, or decisions with a certain degree of accuracy. The system may be confident to a point of 80 percent there is a pet on the image, and 94 percent confident that it is an animal, or 6 percent confident that it is, alternatively, a toy. You may then add on top of the program a feedback loop, which tells the machine whether the decisions are correct.

Both deep learning and machine learning have led to big progress for AI during the recent years. As such, both systems need large amounts of data so as to work, and this is being collected by the sensors, which are continuing to come online through the Internet of Things. The improvement of AI would also drive its own adaptation when it comes to the Internet of Things, creating a virtuous cycle where both areas would accelerate in a drastic manner. When it comes to the industrial side, artificial intelligence can be utilized so as to predict the time at which machines would need maintenance, or analyze the processes of manufacturing that would result in efficiency gains, thus saving millions of dollars.

On the side of the consumer, aside from having to adapt to the technology, the technology can instead begin, also, to adapt to the people. In this way, you can ask the machine to do the task which you require, whether this is searching, typing, or clicking on something.

One of the most useful applications for deep learning, within the geospatial industry, would be image recognition. The systems are trained with thousands of images, in order to detect particular objects, and then learn the pattern of the pixels which are linked with the result that is expected. The technology can then be applied to a number of different levels and would have an effect on the efficiency of the industry. However, image recognition seems to be just a part of the entire consideration.

Deep learning, machine learning, and other AI approaches have been changing many particular themes within the geospatial industry. Some of the areas which need the analysis of location are based on big data, for pattern recognition as well as data modeling. The more data that is generated, the more help with understanding and interpretation that is needed. The potential for artificial intelligence approaches for the industry is quite big, and one should not be afraid to utilize it. In the next two or three decades, the majority of simple and manual tasks related to surveying or map making could be done through or by robots. This would make life much easier, although the majority of the work would still have to be done by people.

Neural networks

From the earliest instances of pattern recognition, the objective of specialists has been to supplant the extent that engineered highlights with multilayer systems need to be prepared. In spite of its straightforward approach, the arrangement was not sufficiently understood until the 80s. It would appear the multilayer designs could be prepared through the basic stochastic drop. Insofar as the modules are smooth elements of the info and their inner weights, an individual might have the capacity to register the slopes, with the utilization of back-propagation. The way that it could be actualized, and that it could become compelling, was observed to be freely validated by various studies dealing with a similar idea amid the 70s and the 80s.

This technique for back-propagation for processing the slope of the target work, such as for the weighting of the multilayer heap of modules, is only a handy utilization of setting the chain lead as it relates to subordinates. The fundamental knowledge depends on the subsidiary of the target, with regards to the contribution of the entire module, and can be determined through working backward from the slope, as one would for the output of the specific module. This back-propagation condition can be connected more than once, so as to engender the inclinations of the function through the majority of the modules, by starting with the output as greater than the base. At the time that the initial angles have been ascertained, this starting point is arbitrary, but the difficulty arises from registering the subsequent points, with deference to the weights for each as the larger contribution of the modules.

A number of uses relating to deep learning, use feed-forward neural system credits that figure out how to delineate the settled-size sort of contribution to the settled-size output. While going through the process, starting with one layer and then moving on to the next, an arrangement of groupings registers a weighted total of the contributions from the past layer, thus compounding the outcome through a non-straight kind of capacity. The most prevalent non-direct capacity would be the redressed straight unit that is the half-wave rectifier and is a component of z = max (z, 0).

In prior iterations, the neural nets used more direct non-linearities, including the tanh, however, the ReLU normally learns at a speedier rate in systems that have only a few layers, and this takes into consideration the preparation of a deep supervised system, without unsupervised pre-preparing. The units that are not in the information or output layer, at that point, would be traditionally named concealed units. These can be viewed as a mutation of the contribution to a non-linear process, so the groupings may still remain distinguishable through to the last layer.

Meta Model

Deep learning can conceptually be thought of as entailing a computational graph made through layers with other layers. A lot of introductory texts on the subject give emphasis on the individual neuron, though in practice, it relates to the collective behavior and interaction of a number of neurons across layers, which is more important. From the perspective of abstraction, the layers of computational units, as opposed to individual neurons, are a correct abstract on the way to understand deep learning.

As such, the largest search engine, Google's Tensor Processing mUnit, gives evidence of this perspective. Unlike the usual CPUs, which treat the scalars and vectors as commonalities, this design treats the matrices themselves as primitive. These layers are constructed on a computational format, whose main purpose is the orchestration of the computation of the forward and backward phases within the network. From the perspective of the optimization of performance, this would be a significant abstraction for someone to have. On the other hand, it is not at the ideal level for one to reason how it would work. It is similar to plumbing, though. To aid the understanding of laymen, one can pretend that it does not exist. The deep learning frameworks have developed over time, to create models which allow for the construction of deep learning architecture.

Questions

- What is deep learning?

- Differentiate between deep learning, machine learning, and artificial intelligence?

- What is the relationship between machine learning and deep learning and the histories involved?

Chapter 2:
Deep Learning Frameworks

"I think people need to understand that deep learning is making a lot of things, behind-the-scenes, much better. Deep learning is already working in Google search, and in image search; it allows you to image search a term like hug."
- Geoffrey Hinton, Google

The machine learning paradigm is evolving over the course of time and has been shifting towards the development of machine learning models which run on mobile, so as to make the applications that much more capable of executing their functions. Deep learning allows for the system to solve complex problems in a timely manner. Considering deep learning is essential to the execution of tasks at a higher level of excellence. Their deployment in a successful manner proves to be quite hard for data scientists across the globe. At the present, there are several frameworks available which allow people to develop tools which are able to offer better abstraction, along with simplification of hard programming issues. When comparing the frameworks, one realizes that each is constructed in a different manner, for a different task. The following illustrates some of the most common frameworks and where each would fit.

TensorFlow

This is probably the best known, and arguably one of the best performing deep learning frameworks, which has been adopted by several corporate giants like IBM, Twitter, and Airbus. The most well-known case of using TensorFlow is probably Google Translate, where it is combined with several other capabilities, including natural language processing, text summarization, and handwriting recognition, as well as forecasting and tagging. It can be accessed both on mobile and desktop and supports languages such as C++ and python, in order to create deep learning models. However, TensorFlow has been reported to be far too complex to utilize it without any interface. The other criticism of the system would be that it runs slower, as compared to some of the other significant frameworks. On the other hand, it does offer developers a faster programming style.

This framework does come available with two significant tools, and these would be:

- TensorFlow serving, for quick issuing of new algorithms while retaining the server architecture and APIs. It also gives different integration with other TensorFlow models. This feature is different from the other conventional practices and can be extended so as to serve other models and data types.

- TensorBoard, for the effective data visualization of network modeling and performance.

PyTorch

Torch is a scientific computing approach which permits wide help for the machine learning calculations. It is known as the Lua based deep learning framework, which can be widely used among the social media giants as well, including

Twitter and Facebook. It uses CUDA and C++ libraries for the means processing, and was made to scale the production of building models, and give an overall flexibility. PyTorch has seen a high level of adoption within the learning framework consensus and is seen to be one of the main competitors to TensorFlow, next to Caffe. As such, it is basically a port to the Torch deep learning framework, for the purposes of constructing deep neural networks and executing tensor computations, which are high in terms of complexity. PyTorch runs using the python language, though, and that would mean anyone with a basic understanding can get started on their deep learning models. Considering the architectural style of PyTorch, the complete deep modeling process is simpler and more transparent, as compared to Torch.

Caffe

Caffe refers to one of the most renowned deep learning frameworks, which can be supported with interfaces including python, C++, and Matlab. It is known for its ability to transport and its speed, as well as its application in modeling convolution neural networks. The biggest advantage of using the C++ library would be the ability to access available networks from a deep net repository, the Caffe Model Zoo, which is pre-trained and could be utilized immediately. In modeling CNNs, or the solving of image processing issues, this would be the preferred option.

The biggest unique selling point, when it comes to Caffe, is speed, as it is able to process over 60 million images on a daily basis with an NVidia K40 GPU. That would translate to 1 mms/ image for inference, and 4 mms/ image when it comes to learning. It is also popular as a deep learning network for the purposes of visual recognition. On the other hand, Caffe does not support the fine granular network layers, such as the ones that are found within TensorFlow. The language modeling can also be said to be lacking, so establishing complex layer types would have to be done in a low level language.

Comparing Caffe and TensorFlow

TensorFlow and Caffe2 are respectively developed by Google and Facebook, which both have different strategies for constructing their frameworks. Facebook illustrates Caffe2 as one of the lightweight and modular deep learning frameworks, which emphasize on portability, but still maintain scalability and performance. In contrast, though, Google aims at constructing TensorFlow into an all-in-one solution for a number of machine learning tasks, and so

TensorFlow is more complicated and bulky. They do share similarities in some of their points:

For example, both platforms allow the users to deploy some of the trained models on several servers or mobile devices, without having to consider a separate model decoder or load a python interpreter. Both TensorFlow and Caffe support auto gradient computation, as they utilize the static computation graph and then pre-compile the network, in order to get the optimal training performance. They also both support multiple machine distributed computing.

TensorFlow and Caffe utilize static computational graphs as well, to attain a higher level of performance, and so they are similar when it comes to their coding styles. Every node, including the operators, when it comes to the computation graphs, is a basic tensor. However,

Caffe2 utilizes Blobs for the definition of the container of data, and for a separate concept. The operators take Blobs as an input and the output, and then do the computations inside. The operators are then realized as proto-buf objects.

When it comes to Caffe2, the Net would be the computation graphs, and this defines the architecture of the network as the proto-buf object. The workspace is the venue where the Net and the variables are. The Workspace, as a concept, is similar to Session when it comes to TensorFlow. The difference between them, in this scenario, is the Workspace initializes an object at the time at which it is used. Session, though, needs to be initialized in an explicit manner before it is used to run the graph.

The TensorFlow code follows the graph definition flow, through definition, to session, to initialization, to the session run. When it comes to Caffe2 code, it is comprised of two steps, which are the graph definition to the workspace run. Model Zoo is one of the useful resources for pre-trained models. That would allow for it to do fine tuning tasks on the neural networks, or to do inference tasks with the use of pre-trained models in Caffe2. Caffe2 still comes with disadvantages, especially if the network is complex and big scale, like residual network or Google-Net, and the proto-text file then becomes tedious, and the code is further complicated. As such, it would be easier to write the code in Caffe2 than TensorFlow, in the event that the machine learning task utilizes the pre-trained model and is not complicated.

It is important to note that Caffe2 is much harder to install compared to TensorFlow, particularly for the big amount of the needed dependencies. On the other hand, the installation of TensorFlow can be done in only one line of pip install command. Caffe2 follows a complicated installation procedure, which then increases the debugging time, and this delay could daunt the users away from further interactions. Though, because Caffe2 uses proto-buf objects to represent the network architecture, it would be easier to print out the architecture and visualize the graph in place, just by a net drawer internal function.

However, when visualizing the graph in TensorFlow, the user would have to utilize the TensorBoard. Even though it is strong as a tool supporting the visualization of the graph and the monitoring of the training process through the summary module, learning of the usage, and embedding them within the particular code, actually takes a bit of time. It is quite hard, especially when it comes to beginners using TensorFlow. As such, it would be a bit easier for someone to pick up using Caffe2, rather than using TensorFlow, and to debug for the simple deep learning models. On the other hand, if the neural networks happen to be complex and the project is what is known as research-oriented, then TensorFlow supports a higher rate of flexibility, and TensorBoard would illustrate the advantages in debugging.

When evaluating the two frameworks, besides the documentation and code flow, there ought to also be a user study based on users who have experience when it comes to deep learning, so as to answer survey questions about the overall user experience. The survey would have contents, such as the time it takes the users to install frameworks. The detailed knowledge can be found in such a questionnaire. On average, it takes a lot more time to install Caffe, both on local devices and remote servers.

The other thing is the average score that users give for TensorFlow, which is rated at 4.0, as compared to 3.375 for the documentation from Caffe. Considering the fact Caffe is relatively new as a framework, the expectation is that Caffe would need to appraise its documentation after gathering feedback from users during the future. Finally, three quarters of the users would have a preference to use TensorFlow to construct the CNN models, and about 88 % of the users would have a preference for TensorFlow in order to construct the RNN models.

Whether the users are able to utilize the framework, in order to create their instances, is crucial for the evaluation of capability when it comes to the framework. One of the main improvements of Caffe2, as compared to the original iteration Caffe, would be the finer level of granularity. Previously, the network was built through the unit layer, and if the users would like to build their customized layers, they would have to build functions that illustrated the manner that the gradient has been computed. On the other hand, Caffe2 provides a replacement for the concepts of layers with operators.

In this manner, it increases the flexibility of the networks, thus making it better to come up with customized networks. Caffe2 is a supporter of 400 operators and users that have the ability to define their own operators, through the C++ code, with details concerning the use, input, and output, not to mention the way that the gradient is passed. TensorFlow has the same concept and support with the customizing of operators, in much the same manner. Both TensorFlow and Caffe offer default python wrappers and general test functions for the tests. Even though there could be a few minor differences in the manner the operators are defined, overall, the consideration in the terms of modeling capability between TensorFlow and Caffe appear to be on the same level.

The other point of comparison would be the scalability, help, and support, as well as hardware support. Scalability refers to the concept of running parallel jobs across different machines within a distributed system. A way to achieve this parallelism for faster training and testing, as concerns deep learning tasks, would be to parallel the model, through splitting it into different portions, in such a way as they can be trained on different devices in a parallel format. According to the official documentation for TensorFlow, the users could set up tasks on different machines, and then link each task with one TensorFlow server. The cluster entails the tasks for the execution of the framework graph. Within each of the tasks, there is a master that would create a Session and a worker who executes operations. In order to allow for parallelism on several machines, TensorFlow would utilize the statement, in order to specify the part of the model to be run on a specific machine. At the same time, it allows a 'tf.train.ClusterSpec' that is shared among all of the devices, and an 'a tf.train.Server' event kept within each of the assignments, to make sure there is smooth communication happening between the machines.

On the other hand, there is a lot of information passing, including the activation and gradient values between the different layers in the deep neural networks, across the distributed system, especially when considering model parallelism. The other parallelism method is known as data parallelism, and that has come to be known as replicated training, where the machines within the distributed system train the same model that has different mini-batches of the data. The significant issue in this setting would be to make sure the shared parameters are updated in the correct manner among the machines. TensorFlow offers many approaches, including replication in-graph and between-graph replication. When it comes to Caffe, though, the scalability has been designed to be significant as a feature, and it is well known for multi-GPU acceleration.

The data parallelism is a built-in type of library, which means the users would need to write code so as to realize the model parallelism. At the same time, Caffe2 features come available with built-in distributed training, with the use of the NCCL multi GPU communications library, which indicates that the user can easily scale up or down, without needing to refactor the design. Though, in the case of TensorFlow, the users are required to define this function on their own. In Caffe2, for example, a lot of the built-in functions easily toggle between the GPU and CPU modes, depending on where they are running. As such, TensorFlow is relatively harder to optimize with concerns for the scalability, on account of the granularity. Caffe2 implies it achieves close to linear scaling with the Resnet-50 model training, on up to 64 NVIDIA Tesla p100 GPU accelerators. Though, the actual performance comparison for the two, in the distributed system, is going to be included within the future works, as there are currently not enough GPU computing resources where experiments can be run.

Considering Caffe2 is relatively new, the community size will definitely be smaller, as compared to TensorFlow, and so there will be less online code resources for it. A study that was done in May of 2017 summarized the frameworks utilized by a number of the popular open source network repositories in Github, and so, there were about ten times more TensorFlow users than Caffe2. The statistics of the Stackover-flow posts, which also related to deep learning frameworks, implied that TensorFlow is the leading format for deep learning framework adoption.

TensorFlow happens to have a number of high-level wrappers, including TensorLayer, TFLearn, and Keras ,which allow common functions to be easy to implement because the coding of static graphs is generally considered as not as intuitive as coding the dynamic graphs. Caffe, apparently, also comes with advantages in the existing pre-trained models, that are available in the Model Zoo, and the Caffe2 team allows public translator tools, for easy translation of the Caffe model to the Caffe2 iteration. This is quite helpful, considering there are a number of ongoing projects in the industry which make use of the Caffe models. On the other hand, the translation of the Caffe model usually costs hours. On the overall, TensorFlow is more supported, and so there are more online resources as compared to Caffe2.

In terms of the hardware support, Caffe 2 supports the generic NVIDIA GPU and CPU alternatives, but it is also claimed to be suited for deployment on mobile devices and to work within the low power constraints of these mentioned devices. Caffe2 is utilized by social media platforms, such as Facebook, for fast style transfers on their mobile platform. It is claimed that it can harness the strength of the Adreno graphics processing units, and the hexagon digital signal processors on the Qualcomm Snapdragon chips, in order to achieve this objective. There are yet to be experiments which would confirm the performances of Caffe2, though the library of the framework's package is only 37.1 megabytes, which is a third of that of the TensorFlow library. TensorFlow had recently published TensorFlow lite, to complement the shortage in mobile and embedded devices. At the present, it only comes with support for limited operators. However, future study is needed in order to do the comparison of platforms on mobile devices.

Caffe2 and TensorFlow have thus been compared in a number of aspects, and as a result, neither of them has had dominating advantages over the other. As such, when it comes to practice, the choice between the two is dependent on the particular user's preference. Overall, in the event that the user has a requirement to pursue speed, and has limited space restrictions on the device, then Caffe2 would be the better choice, considering the results of the experiments have shown that it has a significant advantage over TensorFlow when it comes to both speed and space. On the other hand, TensorFlow is quite stronger and more pervasive, as there are a large number of official and third-party resources, debugging tools, and a larger supporting community, which makes it easier for finding reference codes. Therefore, TensorFlow makes for a better framework for the implementation of a complicated or innovative network, as compared to Caffe2.

Questions

- What are the advantages of Caffe framework?

- Which platforms use TensorFlow framework?

- Which platform would you opt for between the two and why?

Chapter 3:
Components Of Deep Learning

*"Real learning, attentive, real learning, deep learning, is playful and frustrating and joyful and discouraging and exciting and sociable and private all the time, which is what makes it great." - **Eleanor Duckworth***

Everything begins with the model which would be a prediction that the deep learning system is going to utilize. Some of the most utilized and basic machine learning models are linear. They assume the output could be illustrated as a linear algebraic relation, which goes to the input that is then fed to the model. An example would be the linear neuron model, which shows how several inputs are fed into the neuron and then passed as output. When it comes to deep learning, the neurons like this makeup layers, which are stacked over each other, where the input can be the output of a neuron within the previous layers, and the output is then passed on to a neuron that is in the next layer. The role of the activation function would be to make the model non-linear and to compute the values of the hidden layers. A deep learning model may usually consist of thousands of neurons that are connected via the layers.

Deep neural networks and neural networks

The neural network originates from the idea that the neuron's calculation involves a weighted aggregate of the info esteem. These weighted entireties compare to the clear scaling that is performed by means of the neurotransmitters and uniting these qualities in the neuron. The other thing is, the neuron does not simply output the weighted aggregate, considering the calculation connected with the course of neurons would really be a basic direct polynomial math task. Indeed, there is a practical task that is in the neuron, which is performed on the consolidated info. This activity gives off an impression of being one of the non-direct capacities, making the neuron produce outputs just on the occasion the information crosses the edge. Through relationship in this way, the neural networks would apply non-straight capacity to the weighted total for the information esteems.

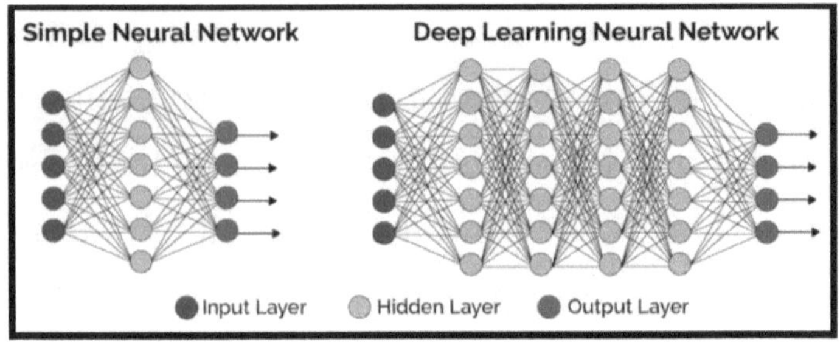

Source: Neural Network [ONLINE]. Available at:
https://www.kdnuggets.com/2017/12/deep-learning-made-easy-deep-cognition.html [Accessed 21 May 2018].

In the principal figure, this is a computational neural network. The neurons in the information layer get some values, and these are proceeded to the neurons in the center layer, for the network which is otherwise called the concealed layer. The weighted wholes from at least one of the concealed layers are then engendered to the output partition, which shows the output of the network to the client. Keeping in mind the end goal to adjust cerebrum motivated wording with neural networks, the output of the neurons would be referred to as initiations, and the neurotransmitters are typically alluded to as weights, which is outlined in the primary figure above. Inside the area of neural networks, deep learning is the place the neural networks have in excess of three layers. At the present, the typical quantities of network layers used in deep learning range from five to in excess of a thousand.

Deep neural networks accompany the capacity for learning abnormal state highlights with greater many-sided quality and deliberation, when contrasted with the shallower neural networks. A case in this situation is the utilization of DNNs, which process visual information. Amid these applications, the pixels of a picture are bolstered into the main layer of the DNN, and the output of this layer would be translated as portrayal of the nearness of various low-level highlights inside the picture, including lines and edges. At the resulting layers, these highlights are consolidated into a measure of the plausible nearness of more elevated amount qualities. For this situation, the lines are joined into shapes, and these are additionally assembled into sets of shapes. At last, considering the majority of the data of the network, at that point, gives a likelihood that the abnormal state highlights would involve a specific scene or question. This deep element sort of chain of command would enable the deep neural networks to have satisfactory execution, in a significant number of the exercises.

Feed-forward neural network

The feed-forward neural type of network, which is also known as the 'deep feed-forward network,' is the typical architecture as concerns deep learning models. The main purpose of the model is the approximation of the function of f*. In this case, this function is a classifier, where y

= f* (x), that finds a category y to the input of x. The work of the feed-forward neural network is the definition of mapping y = f* (x; θ), and to learn the parameters θ in a manner that would result in the best approximation that is there for the classifier. The FNN is the basis for deep learning practices, as they are the main component of a number of deep learning models. These types of networks are usually inspired from neurons and neuroscience, which is where the term neural networks came from. They are termed neural networks as they are represented through a number of functions stacked on top of each other. The length of the functions, or layers stacked together, is what provides the depth to the model, and it is here where the deep learning term originates. An example, in this case, would be the three functions; f^1, f^2, f^3 that could be connected to a chain which then forms $f(x) = f^3$ (f^2 (f^1). Here, f^1 would be the first layer of the network, and f^2 would be the second layer, and so forth, where the input is processed, then passed to the next. The last layer in the model, then, is referred to as the output layer.

The learning algorithm decides on the way it utilizes the layers, in order to produce an approximation concerning f* in the most accurate manner. Between the input layer and the output layers of the FNN, there may be more layers that are referred to as the hidden layers. Every layer that is hidden is usually vector valued, and so the dimensions of the layers would determine the width of the model, where each element in the vectors happens to be neurons, referred to as the nodes. A neuron within the neural network processes and passes on input to the other neurons. The value x^2 that a particular neuron I, in the hidden layer of the second iteration, passes on to the neurons within the next layer, would then be described as

$$x_i^2 = \varphi(\sum_{j=1}^{n^1} w_{ij}^1 x_j^1),$$

n^1 is the last input neuron of the previous hidden layer

f^1, **w^1_{ij}** is the weight

x^1_j is the value of the node j in the previous hidden layer, and **φ** is the activation function.

The concept pertaining to hidden layers needs a function for activation, which is then utilized for the computing of the values of the hidden layers. The activation function is needed for attaining non-linearity, and that would allow the neural network to learn functions that are more complex than a linear regression. A lot of the neural networks utilize an activation function as the non-linear function that then describes output features. The most common for the feed-forward networks would be the rectified linear activation function. When utilized by a unit in the neural network, it is known as the rectified linear activation unit. This would output a non-linear transformation when it is applied to the output of a linear one. A rectifier as an activation function can be relayed as

$$g(x) = \max(0, x).$$

Here, **x** represents the input of the neuron. That is to say, that the function is thresholded at a value of zero. There are several advantages with ReLU, like the fact that it converges faster as compared to the other activation functions, and it happens to be cheap computation-wise, when it comes to implementation. The trouble with the ReLU is it can be sensitive at the training level, causing the neuron to become inactive within the network. On the other hand, if the learning rate is not high, then that occurrence becomes less frequent on average. When the neural networks are utilized for the purposes of classification, the softmax function would be common, as an activation function to utilize the output layer. The softmax function forces the output units, so they are between 0 and 1, though, it also ensures the sum of the output is equal to 1. As such, it is suitable for the classifications, considering the output of the softmax function can be interpreted as a probability distribution. With the use of the softmax function in the classification tasks, it would output a probability distribution for the number of classes within the classification, where the highest value would be the most probable answer.

Convolutional neural network

The convolutional neural network is a neural network that spotlights on the preparing of information with a known framework, like topology. In one example, a convolutional neural network may process the images that are particular 2D arrays, which have the pixel intensities. There are a number of data modalities arranged in several arrays. The signals and sequences are some of the ID arrays, and videos or volumetric images are constructed of 3D arrays. The thing that distinguishes the convolutional neural network from the typical neural network would be that CNN utilizes a type of linear operation, as opposed to general matrix multiplication. The usual convolutional neural network is comprised through different stages. The principal stages are made through two layers, which are the pooling and the convolutional layers. In the convolutional layer, the hubs are sorted out in highlight maps. These are then delivered through open fields, and these navigate over a picture that makes the feature maps. In an element delineate of the hubs, it would be associated with nearby fixes inside the component maps of layers before them, by an arrangement of weights alluded to as the filter bank.

The after-effect of the privately weighted whole would then be run through a non-linear actuation work, like the ReLU. This stage is then called the identifier arrangement. Each hub in the element delineates a similar channel bank. However, extraordinary component maps in a single layer accompany diverse channel banks. There are two reasons why this is the situation. For one, of every 2D cluster, for example, pictures and nearby parts of qualities, usually correlate and form local distinctive motifs. The other thing is the local motifs, like the edges and curves, are invariant as it concerns location, and that means they may appear anywhere within the image. In this case, the convolutional neural network utilizes weights which are shared. The sharing of same weights at different locations may detect similar patterns within a different part of the array of the image. The task of the pooling layers, then, would be to merge the features that are similar into one.

Pooling nodes tend to compute the maximum of a local patch of nodes into a feature map, and this is known as max pooling. Within the pooling layers, sub-sampling occurs and is apparently an advantage for using the convolutional neural networks for the purposes of image processing. Sub-sampling reduces the size of the feature maps, and this, in turn, reduces the number of parameters, though also the significance of exact positions of the feature within the input. During the last phases of the convolutional neural network, the fully connected layers are typically used a lot. A fully connected layer comes with connections to all of the activations which are in the previous layer. They are present in order to let the network learn functions of the previously learned visuals.

One utilizes convoluted neural networks or CNNs to get patterns within sequential data, where there is a direct potential for a pattern, yet, it seems to be hard to place the patterns into words, or extract them through simple rules. For example, the classification of images would be a prime user scenario for CNNs, considering the pixels happen to be sequential, and it is clear to any one, there are loads of patterns. One can try to put into words what separates one image from another, as shown below.

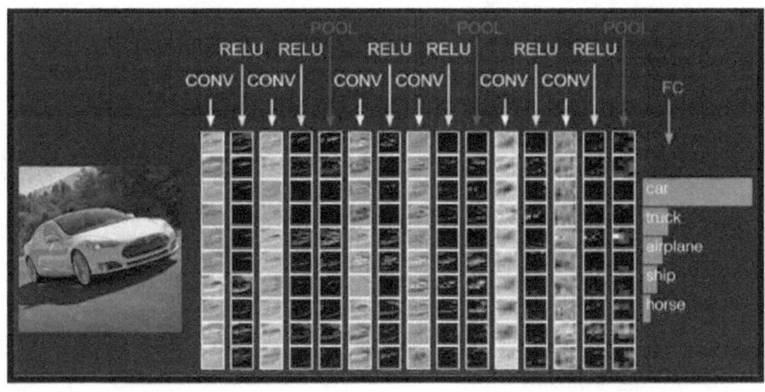

Source: Architecture of a tiny VGG Net [ONLINE]. Available at: http://cs231n.github.io/convolutional-networks/ [Accessed 22 May 2018].

In another example, if a person has sports statistics between two teams, and there is a need to predict the future, then CNNs would be the weird choice. The data provided is not sequential from an inherent perspective. That is, the order is not relevant, and the patterns which are useful have already been extracted. In order to understand the CNNs, they can be broken down into their primary constituents, which would be the 'deep', 'convolutional', and 'neural net'.

Convolutional

Take the scenario that you are blind, but you have an objective, which is to ascertain of which digit the handwritten image is. You have permission to talk to anyone who sees the image, though they are not aware what the digits are. As such, all you can do is ask them simple questions. An approach, in this case, would be to ask questions concerning its formation. 'Is it usually at the top?' 'Does it curve at the bottom?' and so forth. With the sufficient amount of questions, one could actually make a good guess that it is a 7 or a 2. From intuition, that is what the convolutions are doing. The computer is the user that is blind, in this scenario, so it does what it can, and asks many questions concerning the pattern.

In order to make these queries, every pixel within the image gets run through the convolution, which then produces a corresponding pixel, and this then answers one of the pattern queries. The convolutions use filters in order to find the patterns. For example, in the following image, the filter that is above is red on the right and is less red on the left. This filter is essentially looking for the left edges.

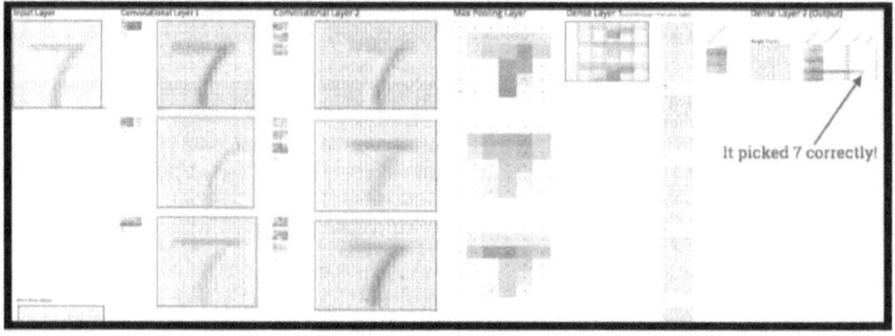

Source: Building a deep neural network in Google Sheets [ONLINE]. Available at: https://towardsdatascience.com/building-a-deep-neural-net-in-google-sheets-49cdaf466da0 [Accessed 22 May 2018].

It is not obvious, at first, why it is going to find the left edges, though in playing with the spreadsheet, one can then see for one's self that this is how the math would work out. Filters may find things that then look like the objects in question. That is how the convolutional neural networks would utilize hundreds of filters. In this case, one gets a lot of scores for each of the pixels, in such a way like a left edge score, top edge score, and diagonals.

Deep

Asking about the edges is okay, though there are questions about complex shapes. This is where the deep multiple layers enter the picture. Now that there is a left, top, and other simple filter of the image, there is a possibility to add another layer, and run the convolutions for the previous filters, and combine them all. As such, the combination of 50/50 at the left edge and top edge could result in a rounded left corner. The serious convoluted neural networks will have several layers that allow the model to build up increasingly abstract and complex shapes. Even after only 4 or 5 layers, the model could begin finding faces, animals, and all sorts of meaningful shapes.

Neural networks

You may say that coming up with the right filters sounds really tedious, and figuring out how to combine all of the answers at the end, to come up with something else that is useful, also seems like a chore. For one, it is great to realize that at the highest level, the CNN has two sections. The first is the convolutions finding useful attributes in the image data. Within the second section, the dense layers combine toward the end of the spreadsheet, and as it does this, it is also doing the classifying. Once the attributes are there, the dense layers are not that dissimilar from running several linear regressions and combining them into a score for each of the numbers. The highest score would be the model's actual guess. Considering the right weights to use for the filters, and the dense layers at the end is annoying. Unfortunately, figuring out these weights automatically is the entire point of the neural networks, so we do not need to worry. Overall, there are two parts to every convolutional neural network. The convolutions, which always go at the start to find the useful features within an image, and the phases at the end, often referred to as dense layers, to classify things according to these attributes.

Recurrent neural network

The recurrent neural network, or the RNN, is a mode of neural networks that is specialized for the purposes of sequencing data. In this case, x 1, ..., xt, where t represents the last unit in the setting. Thus, the recurrent neural network is essentially enhanced by the inclusion of edges which span adjacent time steps. That would mean the sense of time is given to the model, generating a 4D construct. These recurrent edges may form cycles, which are self-referential, from a node to itself, across this axis. At the time of t, a node with a recurrent edge gets input from the current data point from the time step, and also from the values of a hidden node from the previous state of the network. There is a simple set of equations on the way an RNN evolves over the course of time, which is described as

$$\hat{y}^t = f(h^t; w),$$

$$h^t = g(h^{t-1}, x^t; w),$$

In this case, **y^t** is the output of the RNN at time **t**, **x^t** shows the input and **h^t** would be the state of the hidden layer. W represents the weights for the network. The first equation shows that the output at t depends on the hidden layer, and the second equation illustrates that the hidden layer, at this time, depends on the hidden layer at time **t-1** and the input at time **t**. As such, the RNN gets past computations to influence the present computations. The recurrent neural networks have the chance to scale much longer sequences, compared to networks without the sequence based architecture. The main idea about the recurrent neural networks would be to share the parameters across the different parts of the model, which makes it a possibility for the exposure of the model to express different lengths and forms and to generalize data across these parts. With the individual parameters for all of the time values, it would not be possible for one to generalize to the sequence lengths which have not been experienced during the training of the network. It would also not be able to share the statistical strength through different sequence lengths and positions of time. The ability to do this is available when the features happen at multiple positions within a sequence.

Advances have been made in the recurrent neural network architectures, which have deemed them successful when it comes to the prediction of the next character within a word, and a text in a sentence. For example, a sentence can be used, like 'my mother was born in 2004', and 'in 2004 my mother was born'. In the event that these two sentences were fed into a machine learning model that was supposed to recognize years, then it would output 2004 as the relevant part for both sentences, in spite of the order of the words. With a traditional FNN, the task would indicate the network has particular parameters for each of the input features, not to mention the fixed length, and the requirement to learn all the rules of the language in a separate manner at every position of the sentence. The recurrent neural network, though, has the same weights at every phase and is susceptible to different lengths.

Variational Auto-encoders

The variational auto-encoder has been developed as one of the most useful methods for the representation of learning complex data during the recent years. The variational auto-encoders or VAE have already shown promising performance when it comes to complicated data decoding, such as handwritten script, house numbers, speech, and facial recognition. VAE utilizes the structure of auto-encoders, such as decoders, encoders, and latent later. Variational auto-encoders are, thus, probabilistic generative models. The concept was simultaneously discovered by Kingma and Welling in 2013, and Mohamed and Wiestra in 2014. As such, the VAE is a modern perspective on auto-encoders.

The classical image auto-encoder takes an image and then maps it to a latent vector space through the encoder module, and then would decode it back to the output, with similar dimensions as the original image, through a decoder module. It is then trained, through the use of target data of the same images as the input images, which means the auto-encoder learns to reconstruct the original input. Through the imposition of different constraints, when it comes to the code, one can get the encoder to learn interesting latent perspectives of the data. You will be able to constrain the code to be low dimensional and sparse, in which case the encoder would act as a method for the compression of the input data into fewer bits of information.

In practice, the classical auto-encoders do not lead to useful or structured latent spaces. They are not very good when it comes to compression, as well, and thus, they have somewhat fallen out of fashion. On the other hand, the VAE alter the auto-encoders with some statistical modifications, which allow them to learn on highly structured and continuous latent spaces. They have become a strong tool for the purposes of image generation. The VAE, instead of compressing the input image to a fixed code in the latent space, turn the image into the parameters of the statistical type of distribution, which is a mean and a variance. Basically, that would mean that one is assuming the input has been generated by a statistical proof, and the random nature of the process should be taken into account at the time of encoding and decoding. The VAE would then utilize the mean, as well as the variance parameters, in order to randomly sample an element of the distribution and decode that element to the original input. The stochastic nature proofs develop the strength and force of the latent space, to then encode meaningful representations at every juncture. Apparently, every point which is sampled in the latent space is then decoded to a valid output.

When utilizing generative models, one may want to come up with a new random output which is similar to the training data, and this is possible with the VAE. Though more often, it would be possible to explore variations on data that is already present, and not just in a random manner, but in a particular direction. This is the reason the VAE work better than any other method that is currently available.

72

The main issue that is present with auto-encoders for actual image generation is the latent space they convert their input toward, and where the encoded vectors lie is not continuous, and does not allow for easy interpolation. In an example, the training of an auto-encoder is programmed on the MNIST dataset, and visualizing the encodings from a 2D latent space would show the formation of distinct clusters. That would make sense, considering distinct encodings for each of the image types makes it much easier for the decoder to decode them. This is appropriate if you are replicating the same images. However, in the event that one is constructing a generative model, then one does not want to prepare to replicate the same image that was put in. The objective would be to randomly sample from the latent space, or at least generate variations on the input image from a continuous latent space. In the event that the space comes along with discontinuities, and you sample a variation from there, then the decoder is going to generate an output that is not realistic. The reason is that the decoder does not know how to handle that region of the latent space. During training, it did not see encoded vectors from this part of the latent space.

Variational encoders, on the other hand, have latent spaces which are continuous and allow for random sampling. This is achieved by making the encoder not output an encoding vector of the size n, rather, outputting the vectors that are not of size n. There are also vectors of the mean, which are statistically depicted as μ, and the standard deviation depicted as σ. These go on to form the parameters of the vector of random variables of the length, with the last element of the mean and the standard deviation of the last random variable. X represents from where the sample begins and obtains the sample encoding, which is then passed onwards to the decoder. This is illustrated in the figure below.

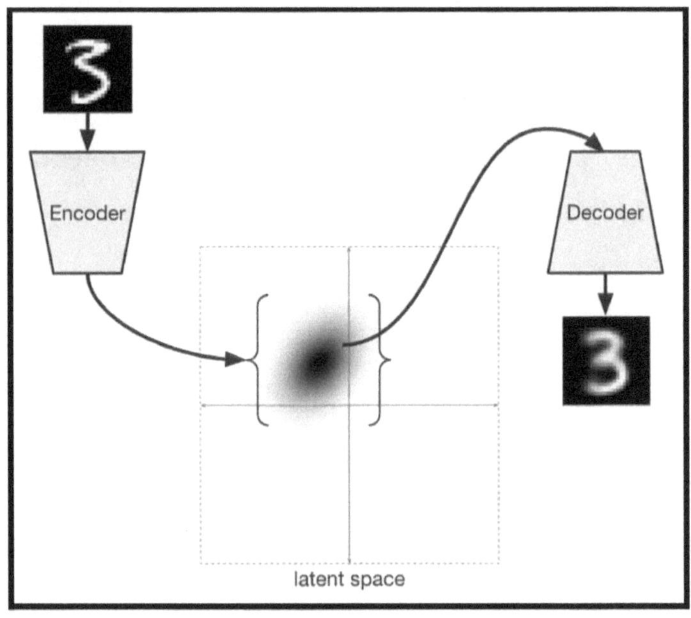

Source: A variational autoencoder [ONLINE]. Available at: http://ijdykeman.github.io/ml/2016/12/21/cvae.html [Accessed 24 May 2018].

The stochastic generation is an indication that even for the same input, though the mean and the standard deviation are the same, the main encoding is going to be different for every pass because of sampling. From an intuitive point of view, the mean vector controls the encoding of the input as to where it ought to be centered, while the standard deviation controls the area since, from the mean, the encoding can vary. As the encodings are generated at random from any place within the cycle, the decoder learns that not only is a single point in the latent space set to a sample of that phase, but all of the nearby points are set to the same parameters, as well. That would allow the decoder not only to decode single particular encodings in the latent space but also ones that vary slightly, as this takes into consideration that the decoder is exposed to a range of variations coming from the same input at the time of training.

The model becomes exposed to a particular degree of local variation through variance in the encoding of any one sample, and this results in smooth latent spaces on the local scale, for the similar samples. Ideally speaking, the objective is to overlap between the samples that are not very similar, in order to interpolate between the classes. On the other hand, considering there no limits on what values the vectors of the mean and the standard deviation take on, the encoder may learn to generate very different means for different classes, thus clustering them apart, and minimizing the standard deviation. That makes certain the encodings do not vary a lot when it comes to the sample. This also implies less certainty when it comes to the decoder. It further allows the decoder to efficiently reconstruct the training data.

The ideal in this setting would be a set of encodings, all of which are as close as possible to each other, while still remaining distinct enough to allow for smooth interpolation, as well as the enabling of the construction of new samples. To force this event, there is the Kullback- Leiber divergence into the loss of function. The KL divergence between probability distributions serves to measure how much the sets diverge from each other. It minimizes the distribution parameters to resemble that of the target distribution. For the VAE, the loss (KL) is similar to the sum of the KL divergences which occur between the component $Xi{\sim}N(\mu i, \sigma i^2)$ in X and the standard normal. This is minimized when $\mu i = 0$, $\sigma i = 1$. From an intuitive point of view, the loss encourages the encoder so that it distributes the encodings evenly around the center of the latent space. In the event that it tries to cheat by clustering them into particular regions, away from the origin, then it is going to be penalized. Using the KL loss data in a latent space results in the encodings becoming densely placed in a random manner near the center of the latent space, without regard for the similarity among the encodings that are nearby. The decoder then finds it hard to decode anything tangible from this particular space, because there is no meaning. The optimization of the two together, however, results in latent space generation that has a similarity to the nearby encodings on the local scale, through clustering, even though it is globally condensed and packed near the latent space origin.

This is the equilibrium which is reached through the cluster forming nature of the reconstruction loss, and the dense packing nature from the KL loss, forming distinct clusters that the decoder is then able to decode. This is beneficial, considering it means that when randomly generating if one samples a vector from the same distribution of the encoded vectors, such as $N(0, I)$, the decoder would just be able to decode fluidly. If one is interpolating, then there are no gaps between the clusters, but just a smooth mix of features that the decoder would be able to comprehend.

The question, however, is still, how to produce smooth interpolations? It should be possible, with simple vector arithmetic within the latent space. For example, if one wishes to add new samples, one can just find the difference between the mean vectors and add half the difference to the original, and then just decode it. The other question is about the generation of specific features, like the generation of glasses on a face. The ideal procedure is to find two samples, one with glasses and one without, and to get their encoded vectors from the encoder, and save the difference. This 'new' glasses vector is then added to any other facial image and then decoded. There are several more advancements which can be made over the variational auto-encoder. One might replace the standard, fully connected, dense encoder-decoder with convolutional-deconvolutional encoder-decoder pair, similar to the aforementioned project, so as to come up with great synthetic human face photos. It is even possible to train an auto-encoder with the use of LSTM encoder-decoder pairs, for the purposes of sequential and discrete data, in order to produce synthetic text, or interpolate between the MIDI samples, like Google's Magenta Music. Variational auto-encoders work with remarkably diverse modes of data, sequential or non- sequential, labeled or unlabeled, and this makes them very powerful as generative tools.

Questions

-    Differentiate between feed-forward and convolutional neural networks.

-    What are the advantages of variational encoders over classical auto-encoders?

-    What are the benefits of the Recurrent Neural Network?

Chapter 4:
Generative Adversarial Networks

"The neural network is this kind of technology that is not an algorithm, it is a network that has weights on it, and you can adjust the weights so that it learns. You teach it through trials." - **Howard Rheingold**

Generative adversarial networks were created by Goodfellow in 2014. In this setup, two differential functions represented by the neural networks are locked within the same setting. The two players are the discriminator and the generator, and they have different roles within this framework. The generator attempts the production of data which comes with a probability distribution. That would be like one trying to reproduce the party's tickets. The discriminator, thus, acts like an arbitrator. It decides if the input comes from the generator, or from the main training set. That would be the party's security, comparing the fake ticket with the authentic ones, in order to find a flaw within the design. As such, the program follows with the generator in trying to maximize the potential of making the discriminator mistake the inputs as legitimate. There is also the discriminator guiding the generator, in order to produce images that are more realistic. In the perfect equilibrium, the generator ought to capture the general training data distribution. However, the discriminator will always be unsure of whether the input is real or not.

The proposed adversarial net structure, which is the generative model, is set against a contender that figures out how to decide in the matter of whether the example is from the model dispersion or the information dissemination. The generative model can be seen as practically equivalent to a group of crooks that are endeavoring to make counterfeit money, and flood it into the framework without cautioning any experts. The discriminative model would assume the part of the police in endeavoring to distinguish the phony cash. The opposition in this amusement drives both of the groups to enhance their approach, until the point when the counterfeits end up indistinguishable from the honest-to-goodness articles. This structure can give particular calculations to preparing for various models and advancement calculations. The motivation behind the structure, in this setting, would investigate the unique instances of when the generative model makes tests, through doing arbitrary comparisons through a multilayer perceptron, and the discriminative model would likewise be a multilayer perceptron. The utilization of this extraordinary case would be alluded to as adversarial nets. For this situation, there is a chance to prepare both of the models with the utilization of very fruitful back-propagation and dropout calculations, and to test through the generative model with just the utilization of forward-propagation.

However, there are no inexact derivations or Markov chains which are fundamental in this setting. It was not all that long ago that most of the work on the deep generative models centered on this point, and this gave a parametric portion to the likelihood of an appropriation of the work. The model would then be able to be prepared by a boost of the log probability. Inside this group of models, likely the best would be the deep Boltzmann machine. These models, as a rule, accompany recalcitrant probability capacities, and thus, they require various approximations to the probability slope. These hardships spurred the improvement of generative machine models, which doesn't especially speak to the potential of these systems.

However, there are currently very few tests which have come out of the dispersive compensation models. The generative stochastic networks are an aspect of the cases of generative machines which can be prepared with correct back-propagation, rather than the variable guesswork that is required for the Boltzmann machines. This work can expand the belief system of a generative machine, through the end of Markov chains used inside the generative stochastic networks. Welling and Kingma, and additionally Rezende, returned with stochastic propagation controls, enabling somebody to back-spread through the Gaussian dispersions with limited measure of difference, and to back-proliferate to the covariance parameter and the mean. These tenets for back-propagation may enable one to take in the restrictive change for the generator, which was dealt with as a hyper-parameter inside the work.

Welling and Kingma use stochastic back-propagation, keeping in mind that the end goal is to prepare the variational auto-encoder generator network with a second neural network. Dislike of the generative adversarial networks, the second network inside the VAE, is really a recognition model that approximates derivation. The generative adversarial networks need separation through the units, which are unmistakable, and thus, they can't model the discrete information. However, the variational auto-encoders do require a type of separation through the units, although these are covered up, and thus, they can't have discrete inactive sort of factors. Alternate methodologies for the VAE exist, although they have a tendency to be less identified with this technique.

Past work has, likewise, thought about the approach of using discriminative sorts of criteria to prepare the generative model. These techniques utilize a framework which is recalcitrant, particularly for the deep generative models. These methodologies are difficult, and sometimes inexact, for the deep models, as they include proportions of the probabilities that can't be assessed with the utilization of variational approximations, and this brings down the bound of the likelihood. Noise contrastive kinds of estimation, or NCE, involve the preparation of a generative model through learning the weights that make the model helpful, with regards to the segregation of information from a settled-static node dissemination.

Use of a formerly prepared model, like the commotion dispersion, takes into account the preparation of an arrangement of models of expanding quality. This would then be viewed as the sampling that permits the preparation of an arrangement of models of expanding quality. This can be seen as a general adversarial component that can be contrasted, and the formal rivalry would be used inside the adversarial network's framework. The primary impediment for the NCE would be that the discriminator is characterized through the proportion of the likelihood densities to the commotion densities of the static dissemination and the model appropriation, and thus it needs the capacity to assess and back-proliferate through both of the densities.

A portion of the past work has used the fundamental idea of having two neural networks contend. The most important work in this situation would be consistency minimization. Here, each concealed unit inside the neural network is prepared to be diverse, when contrasted with the output of the second network, which predicts the estimation of that shrouded unit thinking about the estimation of the other shrouded units. The work is not the same as consistency minimization in huge ways.

For one, the opposition happening between the networks is the sole preparation criteria, and isn't adequate, all alone, for the motivations behind initializing the network. The consistency minimization just happens to be an equalizer, which permits different errands, and it's anything but a primary preparing criteria. Secondly, the nature of the opposition is unique. With regards to consistency minimization, the two network outputs are contrasted, and while one network is attempting to make the output comparable, the other is endeavoring to influence the outputs to appear as something else. The output, for this situation, is single scalar. Inside the generative adversarial networks, one network takes into consideration a rich and high dimensional vector that is used as the contribution for different networks, and endeavors to pick out data that the other network may not know how to process. Thirdly, the determination of the learning procedure is unique. Consistency minimization can be portrayed as an issue identified with advancement through the target capacity, which is to be limited while learning approaches the base of the goal work.

The generative adversarial network is based by a mini-max kind of framework, rather than an advancement factor, and becomes accessible with a target result where one specialist looks to boost and alternate limits. The diversion, at that point, ends at a seat point that is the base concerning the player's technique, and the greatest regarding the system of the other player. Generative adversarial networks, now and then, have been mistaken for the comparative idea concerning the adversarial cases. The adversarial cases are found using inclination construct enhancement, specifically in light of the contribution to the arrangement network. That implies keeping in mind the end goal, to discover the illustrations that can be contrasted with the information, yet, they are misclassified. This is diverse when contrasted with the present work, in light of the fact that the adversarial illustrations are not systems that prepare the generative models.

All things considered, the adversarial cases are basically investigations apparatuses that show that neural networks act in fascinating conduct, and frequently, in a specific way, as they order two pictures in an alternate way with high certainty, despite the fact that the distinction isn't discernible to the human perception. The presence of these adversarial cases may suggest that generative adversarial network preparation may not be as proficient as realized and that it is conceivable to make the advanced discriminative networks certainly see a class, without the imitation of any of the noticeable human qualities.

Fully connected GANs

The main generative adversarial network designs used completely associated neural networks for the generator and the discriminator. This method of engineering was connected to the generally oversimplified picture datasets, for example, MNIST for manually written digits, Toronto Face Dataset, and CIFAR-10.

Convolutional GANs

The structure of the framework completely associated with convolutional neural networks is a characteristic expansion, considering the CNNs are appropriate to picture information. The early analyses done on CIFAR-10 recommended it was harder to prepare discriminator and generator networks with the utilization of convolutional neural networks with a similar level of limit, and portrayal quality contrasted with the ones which are used for the motivations behind supervised learning.

The pyramid of adversarial networks gave an answer for this issue through the decay of the age procedure, with the utilization of numerous scales. A ground truth picture disintegrated into a Laplacian kind of pyramid, and a restrictive convolutional GAN would be prepared in order to create each layer. Analysts, for example,

Radford, have proposed a group of network models known as the deep convolutional GAN, or the DCGAN, that permits the training of a couple of deep convolutional generator and discriminator networks. The DCGANs can make utilization of the strided and partially strided convolutions that permit the spatial-down examination and up-testing administrators, to be picked up amid the season of training. These administrators will, at that point, handle the change inside the areas and testing rates, and a key need inside mapping from the picture, to perhaps bring down the dimensional dormant space, as well as from the picture space to the discriminator.

As an augmentation to the co-mingled pictures in 2D, GANs have been displayed that could incorporate the 3D tests with the utilization of volumetric convolutions. Novel items have been orchestrated, and in the meantime, they additionally introduced a way to delineate 2D pictures to the 3D forms of articles which appeared in the pictures.

Source: Deep Convolutional GANs [ONLINE]. Available at: https://towardsdatascience.com/having-fun-with-deep-convolutional-gans-f4f8393686ed [Accessed 24 May 2018].

Contingent Generative Adversarial Networks

The GAN structure was played out to the restrictive setting, making both the generator and the discriminator networks become class contingent. Subsequently, contingent GANs have the advantage of having the capacity to give a superior portrayal to the multi-modular sort of information age. Parallels can be drawn between the contingent sorts of GANs and the data GANs, and this deteriorates the noise source into the incompressible source and a dormant code, that endeavors the disclosure of inactive variables relating to variety, through the boost of shared data concerning the inert code, and additionally, the output of the generator. This dormant code, at that point, can be used for the disclosure of the protest classes, as indicated by a much-unsupervised boundary, however, it would not be particularly fundamental if the inactive code can be assemble situated.

The portrayals accumulated through the infoGAN appear to be significant semantically, when managing complex hidden tangled factors in picture appearance, for example, varieties in the posture, passionate expression, and the lighting of the facial pictures. Inside their typical plan, the GANs did not have an approach to delineate a specific perception x to a vector inside inert space. As per the GAN writing, that would be considered as the obstruction procedure. A few methodologies have been raised in order to reverse the generator for the pre-prepared GANs.

The freely considered Adversarial Learned Inference and Bidirectional GANs give straightforward, however compelling, augmentations, for example, presentation of the surmising network where the discriminators inspect the joint sets. Inside this detailing, the generator would be comprised of the encoder and decoder. They are mutually set in order to trick the discriminator, when the discriminator gets sets of the vectors of (x,z), and needs to decide the combination that constitutes a real output, comprised of the genuine picture test alongside the encoding or phony picture test, and the relating inert space. From a perfect perspective, in an encoding deciphering model, the output toward the recreation ought to be the same as the information. Generally, the devotion of the reproduced information tests integrated with the utilization of ALI/BiGAN are poor. The devotion of the examples could be enhanced, through extra adversarial costs on the dissemination of the information tests and their reproduction.

Adversarial Auto-encoders

Auto-encoders, as expressed before, are the encoder and decoder set which figures out how to delineate to the inward inactive portrayal, and then generates the image out once more. This implies that they take in deterministic mapping from the information space, for example, the pictures into a dormant space, and map this back from the idle space to the information space. The structure of these mappings arrives in a re-creation, and the two mappings are prepared in such a way that the reproduced picture is as close as conceivable to the first.

The auto-encoders are reminiscent of the ideal kind of re-making channel banks, which are utilized as a part of picture and flag handling. Be that as it may, the auto-encoders, for the most part, learn non-straight mapping in both of the directions. The other thing is that, when this is executed with deep networks, the potential structures which can be used for the usage of the auto-encoders are typically adaptable. Training may occur unsupervised, with the back-propagation being connected between the remade pictures and the first, in order to take in the parameters of the decoder and the encoder.

As inferred previously, one typically looks to the inert space with a specific end goal, to have a valuable association. In the meantime, you might need to perform a feed-forward sort of hereditary inspection from the auto-encoder. Adversarial training, however, would give a road to accomplish these goals. Specifically, the adversarial training could be connected between the inactive space and the coveted, earlier appropriation on the idle space. This would bring about a consolidated misfortune work, which is intelligent of both the remaking blunder and the measure of the way the dispersion of the earlier is different, from what is delivered by a competitor encoding network. The approach would be the same as a variational encoder, where the GAN has the part of the KL uniqueness term of the lost work.

Scientists, for example Mescheder, bound together the variational auto-encoding scholars with the utilization of adversarial training, utilizing the adversarial variational Bayes system. There have been comparable thoughts displayed in the instructional exercises by Ian Goodfellow. The AVB system endeavors an indistinguishable paradigm from the one for variational auto-encoders, however, it uses adversarial training destinations, rather than the Kullback Leibler uniqueness. The training of GANs would incorporate the finding of the parameters of a discriminator, to expand the characterization precision, and find the parameters of the generator that maximally befuddles the discriminator, along these lines.

From the ideological perspective, the discriminator is prepared until ideals regarding the present generator come into question, and then the generator is refreshed once more. Be that as it may, practically speaking, the discriminator may not be prepared, until the point when this happens, however, it might just be prepared for a few iterations, and then the generator is refreshed in a synchronous way with the discriminator. The other factor is a substitute and non-soaking training rule, which is normally utilized for the generator. Despite the hypothetical presence of remarkable arrangements, the GAN training is a test, and generally insecure for various reasons. One approach, towards the change of GAN training, is to assess the observational attributes experienced amid the season of training. These manifestations incorporate the challenges which come in getting the combined models to join.

There is, likewise, the generative model, that is tasked with a specific end goal, to create comparative examples for various data sources. The discriminator loss meets rapidly from to the rate of zero, and therefore, gives no way for the vector updates to the generator. Early preliminaries, to clarify the motivation behind why GAN training isn't steady, have been proposed by analysts, who witnessed that inclination plunge implies commonly utilized protocols for refreshing the parameters of the generator and the discriminator are not fitting, when the response to the advancement issue, as postured by the GAN training, really considers it a seat point. Then again, the stochastic inclination drop is typically used to refresh the neural networks, and there are many machine learning programming settings which make it easy to build and refresh the networks with the utilization of stochastic slope plunge.

Training tricks

One of the fundamental progressions inside the training of the generative adversarial networks, for the production of pictures, was the DCGAN structures. This work was the result of a broad investigation done on the CNN models already used inside PC vision, and they brought about various rules for the training and development of the generator and discriminator. Inside the content, there was a suggestion concerning the significance of strided and partially strided convolutions, which are real segments of the compositional outline. That would make it simple for the generator and discriminator to learn great down-sampling and up-examining tasks, which at that point, add to enhancements in the nature of the picture amalgamation. More specific to training the cluster standardization, it was prescribed for use in both of the networks, in order to balance out training in deeper models. The other proposal would be the minimization of the quantity of the completely associated layers, utilized for the expanding of the potential on training deeper model compositions. As indicated by Radford, the utilization of flawed ReLU actuation works between the middle of the road layers of the discriminator, and gives predominant execution on the utilization of the general ones.

Specialists have recommended assisted heuristic strategies for the adjustment and training of GANs. The main element mapping adjusts the goal of the generator in a slight way, to expand the data sum that is presently accessible. Specifically, the discriminator is as yet prepared to separate between the examples which are genuine and the ones that are phony, with the normal middle of the road initiation on the ones that are genuine. The second, smaller than usual, bunch separation would include additional contributions towards the discriminator, and this is an element that encodes the separation between the particular examples inside the scaled down cluster, and the other example shapes. The goal for this is to keep the mode crumple, in light of the fact that the generator is effectively ready to tell if the discriminator is thinking of similar outputs.

The third heuristic trap is that averaging would punish the network parameters, in the event that they digress from running normally on the past qualities, which can help the joining towards specific balance. The fourth virtual group standardization, additionally, lessens the reliance of one example on others inside the smaller than expected clump, through the count of the bunch measurements for standardization, with the example being put toward the start of training. The uneven name smoothing takes into account the objective for the discriminator as 0.9 instead of 1. The smoothing of the discriminator's limit grabbing keeps a discriminator that is excessively sure, which would give powerless slopes for the generator. There was a thought that this had progressed to challenge the discriminator through the expansion of static, and to the examples previously fed by them to the discriminator. Evidently, uneven name smoothing gives an inclination to the ideal discriminator, while the approach moves the manifolds of the genuine and phony examples. However, it is still keeping the discriminator and finding a segregation limit that isolates the examples which are genuine from the ones that are phony. By and by, it might be executed through the expansion of what is named as Gaussian commotion, to both the combined and genuine symbolism, and in this manner, it toughens the standard deviation throughout time. The procedure of the expansion of static to the information tests capacities to balance out the training.

GAN Variants

The motivation behind the GANs is to combine the novel information tests from arbitrary commotion, however, they were discovered hard to prepare, due in part to the vanishing inclinations. The majority of the GAN models which have been talked about require some hyper-parameter tuning, as well as model determination for the motivations behind training. Then again, the less demanding models for training would incorporate the WGAN or the AAE. The last is somewhat simple to prepare, considering the adversarial loss is connected to an essentially straightforward dissemination in the lower measurements, instead of the picture information. The WGAN, then again, has been composed with the mindset that the end goal is simpler to prepare than the AAE. It uses an alternate plan of the training target that does not experience the ill effects of inclination issue.

It might, likewise, be effectively prepared without clump standardization, however, it is additionally less touchy to the choice of non-linearities used between the convolutional layers. The examples that are integrated through the WGAN or the GAN could have a place with any gathering inside the training information. The restrictive GANs give an approach towards the union of tests, with specific client indicated content. It is clear from the different procedures, that the organization of the latent space makes them mean, however, vanilla GANs don't give an induction model, which permits the information tests to be mapped to the latent portrayals. Both ALI and BiGANs give an instrument for the mapping of picture information to a latent space, however, remaking quality indicates they don't really fundamentally disentangle or encode the examples.

Structure of Latent Space

The generative adversarial networks build their portrayals relating the information they have prepared, and making organized geometric vector spaces for different areas. This is one of the characteristics that is imparted to the next neural network models, for example, the VAE and other semantic models. As a rule, the area of the information to be modeled is mapped to a vector division that does not have the same number of measurements as the information space, and along these lines, it is constraining the model to find the intriguing structure in the information, and speak to it in a way which is proficient. This latent space is for the creation purpose of the generator network, and the information at this level of portrayal might be profoundly organized, and could bolster abnormal state semantic tasks. Cases for these would incorporate turn of countenances from directions through latent space, and the picture analogies that have the impact of the expansion of visual attributes, like eyeglasses on to a face that is uncovered.

The greater part of the models for the GAN have a generator that maps information from the latent space into the space to be modeled, however, huge numbers of the GAN models have an encoder which also underpins the opposite mapping. This is a solid strategy for the investigation and use of the organized latent space of the GAN. With an encoder, the accumulation of the pictures might be mapped into latent spaces and examined in order to find the idea vectors which speak to abnormal state properties, including grinning or wearing a cap. These vectors can be connected at scaled balances in the latent space, which would then impact the conduct of the generator. Like the utilization of the encoding procedure to model the appropriation of the latent examples, there is a proposition for modeling the latent space as a blend of Gaussian noise, and then learning of the blend segments that take into account the capability of created information tests, under the information producing conveyance.

GAN Applications

The finding of new applications, with regards to adversarial training of deep networks, is dynamic as a territory of research. There are a couple of PC applications that have shown up inside the content and have been refined. These applications were made to feature a few ways to deal with the utilization of GAN based portrayals for picture control, and these don't outline the potential expansiveness of use relating to the generative adversarial network. The utilization of GANs for the motivations behind picture characterization places them within the format of machine learning, and gives a valuable quantitative evaluation of the highlights achieved in unsupervised learning. The picture amalgamation is still center in GAN capacity, and this is valuable, when the produced picture can be liable to the previous requirements. Super-determination, for instance, gives a case of the way a current technique can be furnished with adversarial loss segments, which accomplishes higher quality outcomes. The picture to picture interpretation would demonstrate the way the GANs give a broadly useful answer for groups of assignments which require converting the inputs into output images.

Image Synthesis

A considerable measure of ongoing GAN research considers the change of utility and nature of the image generation capacities. The LAPGAN model presented various convolutional networks that were in the Laplacian pyramid system, to create pictures in a coarse to fine design. Comparative methodologies have been used with the GANs, working on transitional portrayals, rather than bring-down resolution pictures. LAPGAN, likewise, facilitated the restrictive form of the GAN model, where both G and D networks get extra name data as info. This approach has appeared to be helpful and is presently normal as training for development of picture quality.

This belief system of GAN molding was then stretched out, in order to fuse with normal dialect. In one case, GAN architecture was utilized for the amalgamation of pictures from content depictions, which would be portrayed as turn-around inscribing. A given content inscription of a winged animal, like 'the white with some dark on its head and an orange kind of mouth,' would prepare the GAN to have the capacity to think of conceivable pictures coordinating that content portrayal. Alongside the molding of the on- content depictions, the generative adversarial 'what-where' network, or the GAWWN, conditions the network, indicated by the picture area.

The framework underpins an intuitive sort of interface, where the expansive pictures might be made incrementally, with the utilization of printed depictions of the parts and client provided jumping boxes. The restrictive generative adversarial networks make for the combination of novel examples with specific attributes. They additionally take into account the improvement of devices for natural altering of pictures, like the altering of the haircut of a man inside a picture, or changing their eye shading. It can even modify their age, and influence them to look more youthful or more established.

Classification and regression

After GAN training has been done, the neural network might be reused for the other down-streaming goals. In that capacity, the output of the convolutional layers of the discriminator might be used as an element extractor, with less complex straight models that are fitted over the highlights, utilizing a humble amount. The amount of the portrayals that are unsupervised, inside the DCGAN network, have been assessed through regularized L2SVM classifier to the element vector, as removed from the prepared discriminator. The satisfactory classification scores might be accomplished utilizing this approach, on both the supervised and the semi-supervised datasets, particularly the ones that had been disjointed from the first training information. The nature of the information portrayal may likewise be enhanced when adversarial training incorporates the learning of a derivation component, similarly as with ALI.

A portrayal vector was developed with the utilization of three concealed layers with the ALI encoder and a L2SVM write classifier, yet, despite everything, it got a misclassification rate that clearly was lower than the DCGAN. In the meantime, ALI has seen best-of-the-range classification come about, when the mark data was used inside the training schedule. At the point when the named training is restricted in supply, then the adversarial training could likewise be used, keeping in mind that the end goal is to orchestrate a greater amount of the training tests.

GANs can be utilized as a part of requests to combine the manufactured pictures, while keeping up their explanation data. Through training of models, just on the GAN refined manufactured pictures, the best execution was accomplished on stance and look estimation assignments. Great outcomes have additionally been recorded for forecast and look estimation, with the utilization of a spatio-transient GAN architecture. A portion of the time, the models that are prepared on the manufactured information don't sum up in the most ideal ways, particularly when connected to genuine information. There have been propositions to address this issue through the adjustment of manufactured examples from a source, with an outcome goal to coordinate the objective space with the utilization of adversarial training. The use of numerous GANs with set weights for the combination of sets was examined in comparing pictures tests from various spaces.

Considering the nature of produced tests is difficult to judge in a quantitative way over the models, and the classification errands are most likely going to stay one of the critical quantitative apparatuses for execution evaluation of the GANs, even as different applications for PC vision are investigated to an ever increasing extent.

Super-Resolution

Super-resolution empowers high-resolution pictures to be produced from bring-down resolution pictures, with the prepared model at surmising photorealistic subtle elements while up-sampling. The SRGAN model broadens these endeavors through the expansion of a loss segment, which then sequences the pictures in order, to dwell on the complex of the real image pictures. The SRGAN generator can be adapted on a low-resolution write picture, and afterwards, can construe photorealistic common pictures with four times up-scaling factors. Rather than the lion's share of GAN applications, the adversarial loss is a segment that originates from a bigger decay of work, that, likewise, takes into account the unending loss of a pre-prepared kind of classifier, and a regularization misfortune that empowers spatially reasonable pictures. In this setting, the adversarial misfortune obliges the primary answer for the complex of the common pictures, at that point delivering perceptually, additional persuasive answers.

The customization of deep learning applications may, as a rule, be hampered by benefitting significantly curated training datasets. Then again, SRGAN is effectively redone to specific spaces, which consider new training picture sets that might be effortlessly worked through, down-examining a corpus of high-resolution pictures. This is essential as an idea, practically speaking, on the grounds that the derived photograph has reasonable subtle elements which the GAN produces, and would change, contingent upon the area of the pictures that have been utilized inside the training set.

Source: Editing the quality of pictures [ONLINE]. Available at: http://blogs.articulate.com/rapid-elearning/10-sure-fire-tips-for-creating-your-own-stock-photos/ [Accessed 24 May 2018].

Image to Image translation

The restrictive adversarial networks are suited with regards to making an interpretation of a contribution to the output picture that is a repeating subject, which applies to PC illustrations, picture handling, and PC vision. The pix2pix model comes accessible with a broadly useful kind of answer for these issues.

Alongside learning the mapping from the info picture to output, this model likewise makes a misfortune work which prepares the mapping. This model has indicated compelling outcomes for various issues of the PC vision, which already had required separate machinery, for example, semantic division, the age of maps from aeronautical photographs, and the colorization of high-contrast pictures. A comparative thought had been given the utilization of GANs with a specific end goal, to combine the surface ordinary maps, and after that, guide the pictures to the characteristic scenes.

CycleGAN broadens this through the presentation of a cycle for consistency loss, which attempts to save the first picture, after a cycle of interpretation, and turn around interpretation. Amid this definition, coordinating sets of pictures are not required for the reasons of training. This makes the readiness of information considerably less demanding, and opens the system to a greater group of uses. For instance, the creative style-exchange renders normal pictures in the style of specialists, like Monet or Picasso, through basically being prepared on an unpaired gathering of common pictures and artworks.

Questions

- Define GANs.

- Discuss three GAN applications.

- What are the elements of GAN training?

Chapter 5:
Similarities and differences in large datasets

*"The goal is to turn data into information, and information into insight." - **Carly Fiorina**, **Former CEO of HP***

Classical Machine Learning Versus Deep Learning

In order to attain high performance, deep networks need large datasets. These pre-trained types of networks, which have already been mentioned, were trained on 1.2 million images. For several images, the large datasets are not easily available, and are going to be expensive and time consuming to acquire. For the smaller type of datasets, the classical types of ML algorithms usually do better than the deep networks. From a financial perspective, the deep networks also need high-end type GPUs which are trained in a reasonable time, utilizing big data. These are quite expensive, though without them, the training of deep networks to a higher performance would not be especially feasible. In order to utilize the high-end GPUs in an effective manner, SSD storage and large RAM are needed. Classical ML algorithms may be trained with a decent type of CPU, without needing the best hardware possible. Considering that they are not very computationally expensive, one may also iterate faster and try out different amounts of approaches within a shorter period of time. They are also easier to interpret because of direct feature engineering, which is involved within the classical machine learning, and so, the algorithms are easy to interpret and assess. At the same time, the tuning of hyper-parameters and altering to interpret the model designs is quite straightforward, considering there is a thorough understanding of the data and underlying algorithms. However, the deep networks seem to be very black box, in that even at the present, researchers do not understand fully the inside of the deep networks.

Deep Learning networks, though, have been able to attain accuracies which are beyond that of machine learning approaches in several domains, like language, vision, speech, and games. For example, the graph below may illustrate the image classification accuracy for different approaches on the ImageNet dataset, as the red regions show the deep CNN approach, while the blue indicate the classical ML approaches.

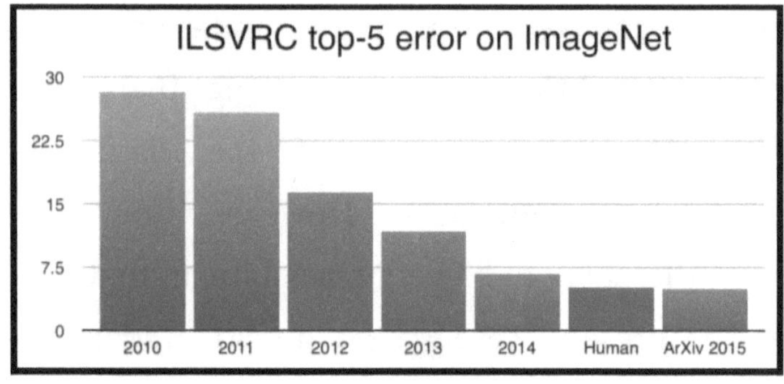

Source: Editing the quality of pictures [ONLINE]. Available at:
https://devblogs.nvidia.com/mocha-jl-deep-learning-julia/image1/
[Accessed 26 May 2018].

From the chart, it is clear that deep learning is far better than machine learning, as it concerns this subject. Classical machine learning algorithms usually need complex feature engineering. Typically, a deep-dive exploratory data analysis is first done on the dataset. A dimensionality reduction may then not be done, for easier processing. The main features have to be selected carefully, so as to pass over the ML algorithm. There is no need for this when utilizing a deep network, as one can pass the data directly to the network and achieve performance right off the bat. This eliminates the challenging feature engineering stage for the entire process. Deep learning methods can be adapted for the different domains and applications, much more easily as compared to the classical algorithms. For one, transfer learning has simplified the process of using pre- trained deep networks for different applications that are within a similar domain.

How they Self Organize

Deep learning neural networks have come a long way in transforming tools for assessment and prediction. There is an algorithm which is known as the self-organizing feature map, which is a duplex network structure that mimics the same structure as most deep learning networks. In this case, it comes with an input layer that reflects the external status information on the competitive layer with weight vector, as the number of nodes within the layer can be limited by the data dimension. As stated, the main building blocks for the SOFM would be neurons. Each neuron is usually connected to other neurons, but the number of these neurons is small. Each neuron connects to a few other neurons that are their close neighbors. There are several ways to arrange the connections, though the most common would be arranging them into a two-dimensional grid. The neurons are arranged in a grid formation, and each neuron within this setting has two properties, which would be the position and connection to other neurons. As such, the connections are defined before network training begins, and the position is the only thing that alters during the training. There are several ways for initializing the position of the neurons, but the easiest way would be to do it in a random manner.

In each of the training iterations, data points are introduced and the objective would be to find the neuron that is closest to this point. The neuron closest is then appointed as the neuron winner. Alternatively, instead of updating the position of the neuron, the neighbors are located. That is not the same as the closest neighbors, though. Before training, special parameters are specified and these are referred to as the learning radius. It defines the radius within which other neurons are considered neighbors.

Applications

Clustering

Clustering should be considered as the most trivial application for the use of the SOFM algorithm. When it comes to clustering, every neuron is treated as a center for a separate cluster. One of the issues with this is that during the training procedure, when pulling one neuron closer to one of the cluster, there will be a need to pull the neighbors in the same vein as well. To avoid this problem, there is a need to break relations between the neighbors, so that any update is going to have an impact on the other neurons. If the value is set at zero, then that will indicate that the neuron winner does not have a relation with the other neurons, which is what is needed when it comes to clustering.

Clustering as an application is quite useful, though it is not very unique. It would seem that the SOFM clustering application is more like debugging. When trying to find where the code breaks, one can then disable some parts, and then try to see if the specific function breaks. In the case of SOFM, some parts are being disabled in order to see how the other things will behave in their absence.

Space Approximation

This is similar to clustering, though, the goal in this setting would be to find the minimum number of points which cover as much data as possible. Because this is similar to clustering, there is a possibility of using the SOFM in this situation, as well. The problem, though, is that clusters are not aware concerning the existence of the other clusters, and they behave in an independent manner. In order to have cooperative behavior between the clusters, there is an option of enabling the learning radius of the SOFM. There is the question of what the use of the application may be. One of the things one can do would be to use the approach for minimizing the size of the data sample. The idea is that since the feature map spreads all over the space that one can generate, smaller datasets will keep the same useful properties of the main one. It can be not only useful for the training sample minimization, but also for other applications.

For example, in a case where there is a lot of unlabeled data and labeling may get expensive, space approximation would be a useful tool. Someone can then use a similar technique to find the smaller sub-sample of the main dataset, and label only the subset as opposed to the random sample.

Someone can also use a more than one-dimensional grid when it comes to the SOFM, so as to be able to capture patterns that are more complicated. As such, the same property of space approximation can be extended to the high dimensional datasets and utilized for visualizations.

High Dimensional Data Visualization

SOFM can be used with two-dimensional feature maps, so as to catch dimensional properties from the datasets with two features only. In the event of increasing the number of dimensions to three, then it would be possible to visualize the result, although in four dimensions, it would become tricky. In the event of using two-dimensional grids and training the SOFM over the high dimensional data, then it would be possible to encode the network as a heat map, where each of the neurons within the network would be presented through the average distance to the neighbors. Between every feature and its neighbor, there are extra squares. In the previous example, each of the squares encodes the distance between the two neighboring attributes. There is a rule not to consider two features within the map as neighbors, in case they are connected diagonally. That is why all of the diagonal squares between the two micro-clusters are colored in black. The diagonals are somewhat more difficult to encode, as we have two different cases. When it comes to visualizing it, there is a possibility of taking an average of the distances. A more interesting way to make this visualization can be with the use of images. In the previous case, we used markers to encode two different classes. With images, there is a potential to use them in a different way to represent the cluster.

Questions

-   Differentiate deep learning and machine learning treatment of data sets.

-   Illustrate ways that deep learning self organizes.

Chapter 6:
Creative applications of deep neural networks

"Whatever you are studying right now, if you are not getting up to speed on deep learning, neural networks, etc., you lose. We are going through the process where software will automate software, automation will automate automation."

– Mark Cuban

Recognition Systems

Traditional movement frameworks for recognition are based on steps which can control and confine the multi-variate, wearable sensor, estimation data. It can be very difficult to decide the data properties which work towards a specific errand, and generally, specific area information is expected to ensure there is significant data preparation. A portion of the regular component extractors can differ from the ghostly illustrations, or basic measurable data, as gotten from Fourier change to kinematic instigated traits, like body stances and body joint position. With the utilization of IMUs, or other wearable assessment instrumentation, the last factor, for the most part, isn't resolved specifically, and should be evaluated through further preparation capacities, including the Kalman Filter. Despite the fact that the kinematic ascribes are near the bio-repairman contemplations, a great deal of the experts would incline toward the factual property extractors of the quick execution, and time to make calculations.

Customary movement recognition, in this manner, puts on a show of being a heuristic approach, which is dependent on the philosophy that was picked, and it includes whether or not extractors have the capacity to show changes between the data streams, for the illustrated forms of data mining. Keeping in mind the end goal to avert episodes of data loss caused by this work process, it might be sensible to use such neural networks which consider an adequate measure of training data, and use applicable qualities of the fundamental data, that would be adapted naturally through the stacking of layers in the changed portrayals of data. The stacked layers would then remain hidden away in the neural network structure, as they ordinarily decrease components of measurements for the principal data structure to a minimal and discriminant data portrayal. This would then ensure freedom from other data enlargement, or ventures to include extraction. A great deal of change to deep network architectures has been made in the course of recent years, and most have been variations of the intermittent neural networks or convolutional neural networks.

Deep Learning in Human Activity Recognition

Deep learning neural network architectures can be used for recognition of human movement data using wearable sensor estimations. A great deal of research has demonstrated the benefit of extensive procuring over the typical element designed frameworks, under the basic data sets of low execution movement groupings, including bouncing, running, and running with both CNNs and RNNs. In one case, a RNN architecture with a huge here-and-now memory achieved 95% of recognition precision on an arrangement of accelerometer data gathered with a mobile telephone. Amid a more broad examination of various network models, both the RNNs and CNNs were delineated to both accomplish better F1, which demonstrates review, and exactness scores, when contrasted with the shallower sorts of networks on multiple open movement recognition data sets. The, then current, CNN structure utilizing one-dimensional convolution along the time-space axis was able to beat the best shallow standard networks by a level of more than 5. All the more recently, a higher precision was accounted for by the presentation of a deep intermittent convolutional network, which had the capacity to beat any of the past networks by around 4%.

Computer Vision and Speech Recognition

Computer vision has been around for some time now, but speech recognition is something of a recent development. Computer vision has led to the advancement of robotics and advanced medical services, not to mention advanced identification methods. There is presently a license plate recognition system which allows the automation of ticketing people who have run red lights or were speeding. Video processing is currently being used to automate scene classification, or answer questions based on an image. Take, for example, "is that a sedan or a bus?" as a question. When it comes to speech recognition, the smart-phone industry has taken over these developments and made them household tools. Both Siri and Alexa are mainstream applications that assist their users with information, appointment making, and directions. They can even look up information at any time and on any subject. Siri is quite flexible and intriguing, considering 'her' ability to understand a number of accents in English, let alone the multilingual settings and abilities, as this is based on several enhancements made in Siri since 2014. These were done through the utilization of deep neural networks, as well as, CNNs.

Deep learning and performance sports data

Research has shown the deployment of deep learning network structures for the purposes of recognition and prediction when it comes to sports scenarios. A lot of these works created network models for the purposes of sport video recordings, initially. Currently, there are not a lot of performance analysis systems which utilize the non-image information in order to learn the deep neural network structures. That would mean at least one system for the prediction of basketball trajectories, one for the stroke consideration in beach volleyball, another for assessment of ski jumping, and lastly, one for the classification of cross country skiing. Because three of the systems are based on wearable sensor data, only their particular system specifications can be discussed in detail.

Internet of Things

This is a relatively new topic which has become quite popular during the last year, because of the changes that connectivity is going through within the tech industry. This can simply be described as instances where common technology, such as the fridge and the security system, communicates with the user. It uses a simple AI which connects the systems and relays information to the user with the use of deep learning tools. As such, it can review the camera footage in order to face-print the visitors and distinguish between the owner of the home and an intruder or friend. It can also adjust the lighting and alarm sounds. The manner the system distinguishes between the parties in this setting can be accomplished through training a DNN, and then a number of systems which can wrap the core detector, in order to give a particular response and action.

Chat Bot

Chat bots may be activated upon the clicking of a support link to an informational or recreational site. The response, which is usually how the system can help the user, is a fully automated tool that evaluates the input text, and then looks for keywords within the description that it has stored inside its answer database. If it is not able to assist, it can also redirect the user to a live agent. As more complex bots are written with the use of DNN, their ability to assess the statements and the context is growing rapidly. They will soon be able to hold more efficient conversations, and may make live agents effectively redundant.

Machine Learning Service Comparisons

Machine learning alludes to an umbrella meaning of computerized and semi-mechanized cloud stages, which cover the dominant part of foundation issues, like the model training, model assessment, pre-handling and further forecasts. Amazon machine learning administrations, purplish blue machine learning, and Google cloud AI are a portion of the chief machine learning administrations which take into consideration quick model training and sending, with practically zero data science aptitude.

Amazon Machine Learning

This is a standout amongst the most mechanized arrangements available and the best fit for due date delicate exercises. The administrations would then be able to stack data from various sources, for example, Amazon Redshift, CSV records, Amazon RDS. The greater part of the pre-performed tasks are done naturally: the administration recognizes the fields which are clear-cut and the ones that are numerical, and it doesn't approach the client to pick techniques for data pre-handling. Forecast limits of the Amazon ML are restricted to alternatives, for example, relapse, multi-class classification, and double classification.

That being expressed, the Amazon ML benefit is in not supporting any of the unsupervised learning implications, and so the client needs to choose an objective variable to mark it in a training set. As such, a client isn't required to know about machine learning, considering Amazon picks them consequently, subsequent to taking a gander at the data which was given. The high mechanization level is both leverage and a detriment for the Amazon ML usage. In the event that one needs a completely computerized, however, restricted arrangement, at that point, the administration might have the capacity to coordinate the desires.

Azure Machine Learning

This is aimed for the setting of an intense learning curve for both the newcomers and experienced data researchers. The program of machine learning items for Microsoft can be contrasted with the ones from Amazon, however, Azure, as of the present, is by all accounts more adaptable, and takes many of the worries out of the crate calculations. The services from Azure can be separated into two classes, and these feature the Azure machine learning studio and the bot benefit. The ML studio is the essential in machine learning, as an administration bundle to consider.

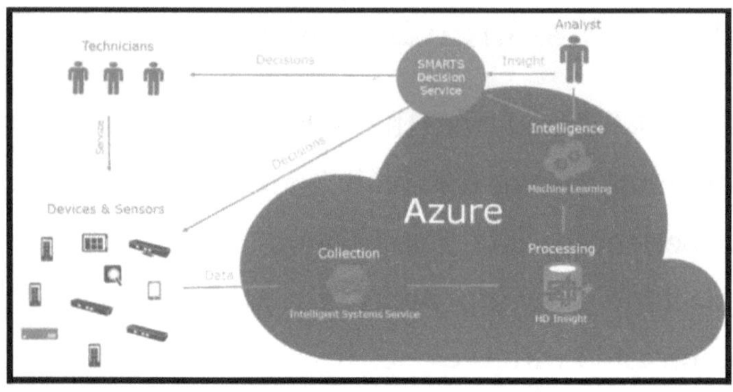

Source: Conceptual diagram by Shash Hedge for Marine LLC [ONLINE]. Available at: https://www.mariner-usa.com/blog/what-is-digital-business/ [Accessed 26 May 2018].

As represented, the activities that occur in Azure ML studio must be done physically. That would incorporate data investigation, pre-processing, and the approval of how modeling comes about. Moving toward machine learning with Azure includes a learning bend. However, it prompts a deeper understanding concerning the primary methodologies inside the field. Then again, Azure ML offers support to graphical interfacing, keeping in mind the end goal, to imagine the means inside the work process. Likely, the principle advantage with regards to Azure would be the calculations that are accessible.

The studio bolsters a few techniques which think about the classification, recognition of the peculiarity, relapse, and proposal. The other piece of Azure ML which is unique would be the Cortana insight display. This is an accumulation of a portion of the machine learning arrangements that have been given by the network, for the motivations behind reusing and investigation by the data researchers. The Azure machine learning item is very intense for starting with machine learning and acquainting its capacities with a portion of the new specialists.

Google Prediction API

Google's AI administrations are given on two levels. This includes a machine learning motor for sharp data researchers, and exceedingly computerized Google Prediction as an API. Notwithstanding, Google Prediction, as an API, has deteriorated as of late, and Google is pulling back its administrations. The expectation API to which it is bound really takes after Amazon machine learning. The moderate approach limits to its unraveling come down to two principle issues, which are relapse and classification. The prepared models might be sent through the REST API interface. The web crawler does not state precisely which of the calculations were utilized for the illustration of expectations, and it did not enable architects to tweak the models. In any case, Google's condition would have been the best fit for running machine learning inside the correct due dates and the dispatch of the ML activity. In spite of this fact, it would appear the item was not as well known as Google had figured it would be.

Google cloud machine learning engine

A state of mechanization for the expectation API was accessible, to the detriment of adaptability. For one, Google ML Engine is the direct inverse. That is on the grounds that it takes into account the accomplished data researchers, and is adaptable while using cloud foundation with TensorFlow as the machine learning driver. As mentioned previously, TensorFlow is a Google item that comes as an open source machine learning library, for various science apparatuses, as opposed to machine learning as an administration. It doesn't benefit a visual interface, and the learning curve for the machine learning driver would be exceptionally steep. However, the library is likewise coordinated with the product designs that are in arrangement with the progression of data science. In that capacity, the mix of Google Cloud Service and TensorFlow infers foundation as an administration, and stage as the administration arrangements, as per the three level models for cloud administrations.

Regardless, it is without a doubt that Azure, right now, has the most adaptable toolset on the MLaaS showcase. It covers most of the ML related assignments and gives a representation interface identified with building custom models. It also has a strong arrangement of APIs, for the ones that would prefer not to nail the data science specifically. However, despite everything, it doesn't have the computerization limits that are accessible at Amazon. Aside from all-out stages, there is the potential for utilizing abnormal state APIs. These feature the administrations with prepared models in the engine, that one can feed data. These needn't bother with machine learning mastery, clearly. Amazon gives multiple quantities of APIs that go for regular assignments inside the content examination. These are mechanized with regards to machine learning.

Amazon Transcribe

This was made exclusively for the recognition of voice and speech based content. It can perceive diverse speakers and even works with low quality sound. That would make it the best choice for the inventor of sound chronicles, journalists, or to help for better content investigation of call center focus data.

Amazon Lex

The Lex API was made to implant the chat bots inside applications, as it has a programmed discourse recognition instrument, and in addition, regular dialect preparing limits. These are finished by deep learning models. The API would perceive composed and spoken content, and the Lex interface enables one to snare the perceived contributions to various back-end arrangements. Unmistakably, Amazon energizes the use of the Lambda cloud condition.

Future trends and tutorials

In the near future, the hardware is going to advance to doubling Moore's law. NVidia has been growing steadily, and should dominate this space as it has throughout most of 2017, because they have some of the richest deep learning environments. Intel's FPGA solutions may also see the adoption through cloud providers, because of the economics involved. Convolution neural networks will also be the prevalent bread and butter for the DL systems, as the RNNs with their current configuration and embedded memory nodes are going to be less so, simply considering they would not be competitive to a CNN based solution. Differentiable memory networks are going to be more common, as well. This is a result of architecture issues where memory will be reconsidered from the core nodes and reside as a separate component from the computational components.

Deep learning is quite easy for those who have coding experience, as opposed to those who are venturing into machine learning for the first time. As such, it would require a fervent effort towards learning certain aspects of the trade. The best way to learn deep learning entails a three step process. The first thing to do would be learning the machine learning basics. That would include data pre-processing, hyper-parameter tuning and more. The next thing to do would be digging into deep learning. The best way to do this would be to delve into tutorial videos on YouTube. Several of these can offer tips on deep learning procedures, especially if one is a novice. Thirdly, one needs to pick a focus area, and then consider it more than others. Natural language process can be one of the fields which would be

used for machine translation, as would
sentiment.

162

Questions

- Name and explain two applications of deep learning.

- What should we expect in the deep learning field in the near future?

- Discuss machine learning service comparisons.

Conclusion

Deep learning, as stated, is an element of machine learning and these are related to concepts such as artificial intelligence and machine learning. Deep learning, it would seem, is advancing the tech industry's field for evaluation and prediction. That would include things like recognizing and distinguishing objects and sounds, learning, and understanding language. In the decades since the rise of computer technology, artificial intelligence has been heralded as one of those all-consuming Holy Grails and has been then thrust into technology's domain. Over the past few years, though, artificial intelligence has developed profoundly, and a lot of this enthusiasm has to do with the availability of GPUs, which allow for parallel processing in a faster and cheaper manner. This also has to do with the simultaneous one-two punch of infinite storage and the data of every stripe, including text, video, and geospatial data.

It can be grouped according to narrow and general artificial intelligence. Narrow AI shows facets of human intelligence, and can do this well, but lacks when it comes to other things. A tool which is great at facial recognition, for example, but cannot do much else, would be such a case. General artificial intelligence, on the other hand, has the attributes of human intelligence such as the factors mentioned on recognition, processing, and problem solving.

Deep learning, like machine learning, is apparently a means to an end ,to achieve artificial intelligence. It makes things more efficient, as it has provided a short-cut based on adaptive response, as opposed to engineering and human programming. As such, one can have artificial intelligence in a tool without having to use machine learning, though, this would need one to build millions of lines of code, complete with decision trees. As opposed to hard coding the software routines with instructions, in order to accomplish every little task, deep learning allows for training of the algorithm, so that it can do things by itself. This conditioning of the algorithm entails feeding it large amounts of data and allowing it to readjust itself so that it can improve.

The text has covered several components and frameworks which have been utilized in deep learning over the past years, as well as their synthesis, which has led to the present tools. Convolutional neural networks and recurrent networks, for example, have advanced the detection and evaluation systems where the CNN-RNN pair is able to feed from a static type of image, and then output a sequence like speech, that would illustrate the content of that image. During an application such as automatic image captions, these systems need to describe the content of the image through the generation of image captions. Both times, CNN acts like a feature that can be trained for the spatial signal. Deep learning has also been utilized to make improvements on aspects of computer vision. Here, one assembles photos, and then would have people tag them. The algorithm would attempt to construct a model which would accurately tag a picture that has a pet or not, as well as a person would. Once the level of accuracy has reached the designated boundaries, then the machine has learned what a pet looks like.

Deep learning also assists methodologies such as inductive logic programming and reinforcement learning, as well as, decision tree learning. Deep learning was inspired through the structure and function of the brain, such as the interconnection of neurons. Artificial neural networks are some of the algorithms similar to the biological structure of the brain. Some functions, such as the general adversarial networks within deep learning, have been instrumental within the assessment field, by utilizing the discriminator and generator approach. The differential functions represented by the neural networks are locked within a game setting. The discriminator and the generator have different roles in this framework. The generator attempts the production of data which comes with a probability distribution. That would be like someone trying to counterfeit the tickets to a party. The discriminator, thus, acts like an arbitrator, and tries to determine the fakery. This has also advanced aspects such as image to image translation. Similar approaches have been utilized with the GANs operating on intermediate representations, as opposed to lower resolution images. This allows image interpretation by the machines themselves, to identify and distinguish images by the way that they appear similar, in the same way that a person is able to differentiate objects from their physical appearance and visual signatures. However, the tool goes one step further, to allow for prediction on certain aspects, like how a person would look in a certain attire, or body type, or even age.

This ties in to the potential applications of deep learning, which have been discussed, and seem to cover the entire current tech industry. This includes biometric identification, facial and speech recognition, not to mention motion sensors. In short, deep learning is currently the foremost authority in the basics of artificial intelligence, because it provides all the currently popular elements for assessment and processing.

The future trends all point to it being the most utilized tool for graphics, sensory systems, and artificial intelligence, which includes robotics and virtual assistance. Now, learning the skills requires a fairly basic amount of knowledge on machine learning and how artificial intelligence works, though, tutorials abound online on deep learning as a skill, and the average timeline to get up to speed to a relatively basic coding level would be six months.

Hopefully, this has all been a help in giving the elementary fundamentals on deep learning.

About the Author

Steven Cooper is a data scientist and worked as a software engineer at multiple startups. Now he works as a freelancer and helping big companies in their marketing and statistical analysis using machine learning and deep learning techniques.

Steven has many years of experience with coding in Python and has given several seminars on the practical applications of data science, machine learning, and deep learning over the years. In addition, he delivers training and coaching services that help technical professionals advance their careers.

He loves to write and talk about data science, machine learning, and Python, and he is very motivated to help people developing data-driven solutions without necessarily requiring a machine learning background.

When not writing or programming, Steven enjoys spending time with his daughters or relaxing at the lake with his wife.

www.ingramcontent.com/pod-product-compliance
Lightning Source LLC
La Vergne TN
LVHW051523170726
843492LV00006B/1601